A Production of Sheepdog Crafts

ChatGPT & Canva

were used in the production of this book.

This playful puppy
is looking for his family.

He is soft, fluffy, and full of wiggles!

The puppy with his sister.

The puppy likes to play with his sister.

At 5 weeks old, the puppy meets Dawn and Bill.

The puppy is showing off for Dawn and Bill.

Oh, he's beautiful!

We have to go, but we will see you in three weeks.

The puppy wonders where Dawn and Bill are going.

The puppy misses Dawn and Bill.

The puppy wonders for three weeks, where are they?

Three weeks later, the puppy is surprised by a sound.

The puppy goes searching to see what the sound is!

They are back! They are back!

Dawn and Bill have returned, looking for the puppy.

There he is!
There's the puppy!

I see him! I see him!

There he is!

Look at what I have got.
I love him!

It is my turn to hold him.

The puppy has gotten big for 8 weeks old.

Watch the puppy run and play.

Should his name be Banjo or Oreo?

BANJO! BANJO!

BANJO! BANJO!

BANJO! BANJO!

I like Banjo. He will be a bluegrass dog.

You will be Banjo, my Service Dog.

Banjo, are you ready to go to your new home?

This will be your home!

At 8 weeks old, Banjo found his new home with his mom and dad.

THE END!

Banjo, The Service Dog

Banjo, The Service Dog, was born June 25, 2017. Bill and Dawn brought him home at 8 weeks old. At 14 weeks old, Banjo began training and became Bill's Service Dog.

www.ingramcontent.com/pod-product-compliance
Lightning Source LLC
LaVergne TN
LVHW070205110826
845147LV00002B/507

* 9 7 9 8 2 3 4 0 6 2 4 5 1 *